Holy Family Church

208
Dau. St. Paul   #111

THE CONSCIENCE GAME

THE CONSCIENCE GAME

The Story of St. Thomas More

WRITTEN AND ILLUSTRATED
BY THE
DAUGHTERS OF ST. PAUL

ST. PAUL EDITIONS

NIHIL OBSTAT:

REV. SHAWN G. SHEEHAN
Diocesan Censor

IMPRIMATUR:

✠ RICHARD CARDINAL CUSHING

Library of Congress Catalog Card Number: 66-29165

Copyright, 1967, by the *Daughters of St. Paul*

Printed in U.S.A. by the *Daughters of St. Paul*
50 St. Paul's Ave., Jamaica Plain, Boston, Mass. 02130

CONTENTS

PART I

How to Begin 13

The Meager Days 16

A Decision 21

Lawyer and Husband 23

"Dear Jane" 28

Henry VIII — King 31

PART II

A Full Time Job 35

What's in a Title? 39

Ambassador on the Homefront 41

Golden Days at Chelsea 43

1525 — A Restless Year 47

Trial in Blackfriar's Hall 50

Wolsey without the Red 53

PART III

New Lord Chancellor 57

Who Shall Hold the Keys: Peter or the King? 61

A Victory for Ex-Chancellor More 63

The Appointment 66

So High the Price 69

The Tower 71

Making and Breaking 75

Cardinal Fisher 77

Persuasion 79

The Longest Road 82

Victory — July 6, 1535 85

PART I

*"What our lot brings us must be borne;
and I have composed my mind
for every event."*

St. Thomas More

Chapter 1

HOW TO BEGIN

Just about the time that Columbus was sailing the blue seas to American shores, one of the most lasting and unusual events had just begun to form in England. A drama which would shake the world of its day and echo down the ramparts of time, even to our own day, was now in the making. In fact, most of the "players" were living and breathing, yet completely unaware.

A new son had been born to King Henry VII at Lambeth Castle. His name was Henry VIII.

The son of an Ipswich butcher, brilliant and grasping, was a student at Oxford. His name was Thomas Wolsey.

The son of a prominent judge, a jolly and impetuous lad of thirteen, was in the service of Bishop Morton; his name was Thomas More.

The daughter of a Spanish king thanked God that her daddy was driving the Moors from Spain. She was six-year-old Catherine of Aragon—"Catalina."

Oh, there were many more actors and actresses, who had minor roles, but the most significant have been mentioned, except one.

The third daughter of Sir Thomas Boleyn would not be born until fifteen years later. But when that day came, she was named Anne.

*

Life was wonderfully interesting in the household of John Morton, Archbishop of Canterbury. Thomas was the Archbishop's page. He was ever present, be it "to pass a goblet or run an errand."

The four years that he was to spend there were to offer so many golden opportunities to learn. They were to be the practical application of the education received at St. Anthony's School on Threadneedle Street. Archbishop Morton was a priest, a diplomat, a father, a friend to the flock of his realm. Thomas listened to him and chalked up his wise answers for the days when, as Lawyer More, he could counsel as well.

Thomas liked a good joke. In fact he liked lots of good jokes, and yet he had to control his love for continual fun, and learn even while young, that everything had its proper time. When he forgot, which was often enough, Judge More knew just how to remind him.

But life was good in the Archbishop's house. When there were guests, group comedy plays were the entertainment, which was customary in those days. Thomas' delight was to jump into the scene, unpredicted, and see himself rapidly become the center of attraction.

❂

Four years sped by. The day came when the fatherly Archbishop assured Thomas that he was quite ready to leave his household and begin studies at Canterbury College, Oxford.

"I will miss you," the lad said quietly.

The old man patted his head of unruly hair. There were tears in the Archbishop's eyes.

Chapter 2

THE MEAGER DAYS

The life of an Oxford student was noted for its rigidity. The accent was definitely on the development of man's mind; on the acquisition of learning. To recall, just in a general way, the schedule of each student, we would have to explain it thus:

      5:00 A.M.   Holy Mass
      6:00 A.M.   Studies began
     10:00 A.M.   First meal
Remainder of day until 5:00 P.M.—lectures, discussions, disputations
      5:00 P.M.   Last meal (only two served daily)
      8:00 P.M.   All students must be in room

The only thing that would salvage the fun-loving More from the straight schedule and lend some pleasant deviations, would be if his father, Judge More, would increase his weekly allowance. Certainly it would be no strain on Judge More's pocket book, and it never even dawned on Thomas that his father might refuse.

"If I increase your allowance, you'll increase your fun to equal it," his father insinuated gently. "I know you too well, son."

"But Dad," Thomas muttered in disbelief.

His father only shook his head. When Judge More said "no," it was "no."

He was upset, but not for long. There was no use pouting about it. Thomas decided to play the role of the "poor scholar," and learn to be cheerful about it! In fact, in due time, he began to love the simple Oxford life. His daily schedule was almost monastic, and he was happy, not because of the austerity, but in spite of it.

He began to notice all the things which might otherwise have passed him by... the fine architecture of the buildings in which he now lived; the gorgeous landscape; the friendship of companions who worked toward the common goal of well-rounded education. But above all, a real love for learning, which had slowly developed in the past, was now fully realized by More and thus he began a quest for knowledge, which would burn even to the last days of his life.

Young Thomas More was part of a group called the Oxford Reformers. These men, John Grocyn, Thomas Linacre, William Lily, John Colet (who later became More's confessor) and others, had a philosophy and the hope of putting that philosophy into action. They saw the honest need for reform, but not as the Protestant Reformers were doing it by separating from Rome, but rather by correcting ecclesiastical abuse and by widening the horizons of learning. "To better the lot of men"; this was the motto of the curious band of men who had plunged, uninvited, into a herculian task—the reformation of the world. Someday, that very motto, "to better the lot of all men," would be the light which would guide Sir Thomas More's writing of "Utopia."

❋

Perhaps it never crossed the mind of Judge More that his son might wish to enter something other than the law profession, which he had just taken for granted. Thomas was completely taken back by the idea. The switch from his Oxford haven to a law school, called New Inn, was a sacrifice to say the least. But, although it cost him more than anyone ever knew, except perhaps a few of his closest friends, he tossed all his energies into the new endeavor. And soon it paid off. He earned the position of READER, which is similar to a University Professor. His lectures were packed to capacity and over-flowing. Brilliance and wit were a combination, which made More a favorite among teachers and students both.

But the break with his Oxford life was not severed completely. Although philosophy and Greek were not a part of the New Inn curriculum, Thomas found ample time for studying them by a method of amazing self-discipline. His sleep was cut to a mere four hours each night, perhaps five. And he really slept on a wide piece of board instead of a mattress. Meanwhile, one by one, his best friends were arriving in London from Oxford. First Grocyn; then Linacre; then Colet; then Lily. Their pasttime was not spent in carefree living. But these "poor scholars" devised their own means of recreation. They imitated wholesome competition in Greek and Latin, educational as well as economical.

Thomas More was an educated man when he emerged from law school. There was plenty of opportunity in England for his skill and wit. True, there were a few more years of schooling left. Yet, he had another problem all his own furrowed deep in the pit of his soul. This must be tackled first. There was a solution; he knew there was. A decision would be called for. He knew that too. So now it was time to call that *problem* to the front line and **win.**

Chapter 3

A DECISION

The Carthusians, an austere Order of Monks, in the long history since their foundation, had never experienced the need for reform. For a long time now, More had looked upon these men from a distance, and could not brush aside the goodness of their rigid lives. Always the monastic life had appealed to him. He had learned to love the silence, the prayer, the studies, the fatiguing labor from the time of his student days at Oxford.

Now it was Judge More's turn for a surprise. Quite suddenly, Thomas moved from his campus home to a place called the "London Charterhouse" staffed by the Carthusians. This was not really a hasty move. It had taken a lot of thought. He had not entered the Order; there were no vows taken. But he followed their rigorous schedule, participated in all the religious exercises and mortifications; yet he continued his schooling in law.

For the three years that he spent there, Thomas searched his own soul and the monastic life he had chosen. Some say it was the question of celibacy; others say that his confessor advised him. But perhaps he left the Charterhouse after much self-examination—for with it might come the awesome realization that although he loved the monastic way of life, he had to admit that it was a vocation, and he had not been called. Whatever the reason, Thomas More resumed his role of layman with peace of mind, assured that now he was on the right road.

CHAPTER 4

LAWYER AND HUSBAND

This was the time for adjustment in the life of Thomas More. His law practice was growing rapidly. His friendliness towards everyone and love for justice soon carried his reputation throughout London. He never did learn to say "no" to anyone. It was impossible to think that he would refuse a favor. Inconvenience borne for the sake of others takes virtue—and virtue is acquired. No one really knew of the countless acts of self-denial that this man practiced each and every day. Perhaps his stearnest mortification was the painful hairshirt, worn next to his skin, which was completely hidden from view. In hot weather, it could be terrible, and yet it was remarkable what a smile could hide.

The personal side of his life was blooming, too. Sir Thomas More was twenty-seven years old and his young bride, Jane Colt, was just seventeen. Someone described her as "a country miss from Essex."

Everything was overwhelming to young Jane. She didn't understand her scholarly husband and his high-brow friends who came to visit. She didn't like his educated jokes and many talents. And she missed home and her mother and father.

Tears were forever welling in her eyes and sliding down her pale cheeks with the slightest provocation. Thomas tried to correct her. He tried to demonstrate the method of intelligent conversation. But the advice was not well received. Finally he became aware of the fact that he just had to tell her father. Perhaps he would have a solution to the problem.

"Use your rights," he told Thomas. "Give her a good beating."

Thomas laughed heartily at the drastic suggestion and mumbled that he just couldn't do it. So Mr. Colt had a private conversation with his young daughter.

"Grow up," he demanded. "You are a disgrace to your mother and me." And the scolding continued for what seemed to be eternity.

LAWYER AND HUSBAND

Never had Jane seen her mild-tempered father so furious. She quickly decided that rather than return home, life would be much more bearable by making a home for her understanding husband.

Their love for each other blossomed into almost an idyllic happiness. The couple were thrilled with the anticipation of their first child. During the months of waiting, Jane joyfully took music lessons from her talented husband.

•

One man who frequently visited the More family, and knew them intimately, was a Dutch scholar named Erasmus.

Thomas and Erasmus had met in the home of London's Lord Mayor:

"You must be More or no one," Erasmus said when they were introduced.

"You must be Erasmus or the devil," More retorted. Thus two men, who were destined to become the best of friends, met.

It is from the talented pen of Erasmus that we get the first of many biographies of Thomas More. Erasmus grew to love his friend and remained in awe at his virtues. Some of his comments about Sir Thomas are,

"You must be More or no one," Erasmus said....

"I have never seen a person less fastidious in his choice of food.... He likes to be dressed simply.... He seems to be born and made for friendship of which he is a sincere and persistent devotee.... If he has fallen in with anyone whose faults he cannot cure, he finds some opportunity of parting with him, untying the knot of intimacy, without tearing it."

CHAPTER 5

"DEAR JANE"

It was not only his friends who loved him. His ever increasing family loved him too—Margaret, Elizabeth, Cecilia, and the baby, John—these were the objects of his happiest moments. Only God could see the cloud which was soon to cover the happy group. When little Meg was five years old, and John near his first birthday, the sweet-natured wife of Sir Thomas died. It was a shock and sorrow that this man would carry for the rest of his life. On her tombstone, he had written,

"Dear Jane, Thomas More's little wife"

Mistress Alice Middleton, a widow seven years older than Thomas More, was a practical, efficient, almost cold woman, staunchly loyal and really kind in her own sort of way. Sir Thomas was alone with four small children to raise. His hours of Law practice would never permit his being a father and mother as well.

Lady Alice understood this and married him, taking on the responsibility of his four children, generously and totally.

There would never be another Jane in his life—the love of his youth, the sharer of his most secret dreams. No one was more aware of this than his second wife and yet Lady Alice would win his grateful affection for the excellent upbringing she would impart to his children.

*

Sir Thomas More had definite ideas when it came to the education of his children. First of all, they were educated right at home. The best of tutors were brought in. Secondly, completely contrary to the opinion of the day, Sir Thomas staunchly believed in the education of women. His three girls received a thorough and humane education. Over the years, they became saturated with theology, philosophy, Greek, Latin, logic, mathematics and astronomy. They were all good pupils, but especially Meg. The bond that grew between Sir Thomas and Meg would never break. She was his favorite, the one who now understood him the most, and the feeling was quite mutual. Only she knew of the hairshirt that he wore. In fact, it was she who washed it for him. Lady Alice did not know, nor could she have understood such things.

Chapter 6

HENRY VIII—KING

The death of Henry VII, on the twenty-first of April, 1509, was not heavily mourned by the nation he had ruled. In fact, almost all of England looked ahead with joy and expectation at the New Era soon to begin. Even the scholarly friends of More expected much advancement in English learning. The hopes of the nation were placed in the pocket of an eighteen year old prince, who was described by More as,

"Tall and handsome, rich in intellect, rich in power, rich in purse, eager for learning, eager for justice...." Such was the description of England's new king, Henry VIII.

The woman who was soon to become his queen, the Spanish Catherine of Aragon, was the object of Sir Thomas' pen also,

"There is nothing wanting in her, that the most beautiful girl should have."

And so it would seem that England's future promised to be a glorious one.

Besides the flourishing law practice, Sir Thomas fulfilled a task, which he loved very much. He was Under-Sheriff of London. With the activity, which flooded his life, a prayer-life to match it, flourished. Daily Mass, oral prayers and psalms recited with the entire household, numerous mortifications known only to Meg—these furnished the spiritual strength which ruled his life.

And when there was a spare moment here and there, the gifted pen of Thomas More sprang into action. "Richard III" was begun about this time.

The year was 1515. Thomas Wolsey had now been raised to the Cardinalate. He was always at the side of young Henry VIII, whispering ideas...plans...and schemes. And Wolsey had the skill and brains to make them a reality. Gradually he had organized a tremendous army and fleet. Henry was momentarily distracted from learning and the arts. Now he was aglow with the "Valiant Warrior" prospects. Meanwhile, Wolsey was ever present, insinuating, suggesting and planning....

PART II

*"A man is more precious
for what he is,
than for what he has."*

CONSTITUTION ON THE CHURCH
IN THE MODERN WORLD

Chapter 1

A FULL TIME JOB

It wasn't especially that Wolsey had any particular liking for him. Rather, it was because he needed him; his goodness, his interpretation of the Law, his eloquent command of every situation. That was why Sir Thomas More was called into the royal service. Erasmus and all his intellectual friends moaned, that now the poor man would never have time to engage in literary pursuits. But Thomas More knew how to squeeze the most into a day; or should we say, out of a day.

Ambassador More's first assignment took him to Flanders in 1515. There were difficulties to settle between the merchants of England and Flanders. More hated to leave his home, his family and the law practice, but he felt that it was a duty to go. So pushing aside personal preference and assured that the family would progress, he went. The project was expected to last sixty days in all. Instead he stayed six months.

During the long evening hours and far into the night, Sir Thomas put his pen to good use. In fact, here was begun his great work "Utopia," which was published the following year in 1516. Utopia was not written in English, for fear that the unlearned would be misinformed and confused.

"I would burn my books with my own hands," More declared, "rather than have folks receive harm from them."

＊

He was grateful to be back in England again. His law practice had been necessarily neglected and work was impatiently waiting and piling up on his desk.

One of the first cases that Sir Thomas was called to defend was startling indeed. The incident involved a Papal ship, which was accused of illegally pulling into Southampton Port. More represented the Papal Nuncio. Even the King attended... and Wolsey. More won brilliantly.

＊

May Day, 1517, found London in an ugly mood. Prejudice against foreigners,–Italians,

A FULL TIME JOB

Flemish and Frenchmen—soared high, because they were stealing the business from English craftsmen.

The crowd milling in the street was fast growing into a mob. More, alone, had the courage to face them, challenging them to meet "fury with common sense." They cursed and shouted but did no more than that. Toward morning, the crowd gradually dispersed and order was restored. It was Thomas More, his prestige among the common men, which had stayed the riot before it grew into rebellion. Cardinal Wolsey was quite aware of it. "Henceforth, there could be no alternative. All the hours of this wise man, this respected man, this good man, must be given the king." [1]

These two completely successful endeavors brought about the inevitable. Sir Thomas More was now invited into the King's employ, on a full-time basis. The only one really happy about it was his wife, Alice.

"It is far better to rule than be ruled," she quipped.

"In all truth, wife," More teased, "in this you speak the truth, for I have never found you willing to be ruled yet."

---

[1] *The Story of Thomas More*, John Farrow; All Saints Press, p. 61

The youthful King was delighted with the wit and sparkle lent to the conversation by Sir Thomas More. It got so bad—in fact, Sir Thomas saw his family so little—that he decided to try his best to become "dull" so as not to be so much in demand. He did eventually get called upon less because Henry realized he was a family man. But Thomas More never did succeed in becoming boring.

When Charles, King of Spain, was expected to arrive for a visit, many of the arrangements were given to More to handle. This required that he work almost side by side with Henry. The two became very close and Sir Thomas began to know his King very well. He became Councillor and Royal Secretary while Wolsey, on the other hand, surrounding himself in glitter, compliments, bribes and honors, became isolated in his own grandeur.

A short time later, Lady Alice learned that her husband would be traveling again. This time he must accompany King Henry to France. Henry's party arrived in Calais and there was met by Emperor Francis and the group traveling with him. Thus, there was a happy note for Sir Thomas after all. Erasmus, his best friend, was among the Emperor's party. The two friends met again. What a marvelous conversation followed.

Chapter 2

WHAT'S IN A TITLE?

The Doctrinal Revolt against the Church, which was slipping into many countries, had not so much as an ounce of a hold in England. In May of 1521, a huge bonfire fed by the books of Luther raged in St. Paul's Church yard. Cardinal Wolsey had planned the demonstration. The sermon for the occasion was delivered by John Fisher, Bishop of Rochester. Henry VIII was so impressed with the sermon that he ordered it translated into Latin and preserved.

At this time, a scholarly book entitled "Assertion of the Seven Sacraments," was written by the King, Henry VIII. But it was not a task that he accomplished alone. Sir Thomas acted somewhat like the editor, or as he put it, "a sorter outer and placer of the principal matters, therein contained." Ambassador John Clark presented the book to a grateful Pope, Leo V, who replied to Henry,

"We, the true successor of St. Peter... bestow on your Majesty this title, 'Defender of the Faith.'"

Chapter 3

AMBASSADOR ON THE HOMEFRONT

Meg, the family favorite, was married now. Her husband, William Roper, met all the requirements of a good husband, except one. Through his contacts with the German merchants of the steelyard, he had become infested with current heresies and had put aside his own Faith for a while. So loud was he on matters of religion, that reports of "heresy" had reached the ears of Wolsey. The Cardinal called Roper in, but because of his father-in-law, Roper was only warned. His public arguments became less noisy, but his opinion was firm.

Sir Thomas had spent many long hours trying to reason with his perplexed son-in-law. He had argued, debated, answered all questions brilliantly. But Roper stood firm.

At last Sir Thomas mumbled to Meg in exasperation:

"I have borne a long time with your husband. I have reasoned and argued with him on points of religion, and given him my poor fatherly counsel, but none of this has called him home. Therefore, Meg," he said with determination, "I will no longer argue and dispute with him, but will pray to God for him."

Prayer certainly succeeded where eloquence had failed. Young Roper soon returned to the Faith and totally devoted himself to Catholicism, from which he never strayed again.

*

But an incident which took place in the King's court, did not have such a happy conclusion. Lord Percy, one of the many young Englishmen, fell quite unpredictably in love with one of Queen Catherine's maids-in-waiting. Romance between nobility and commoners was frowned upon, especially by Wolsey. He was quite harsh in telling Lord Percy to end the romance. The young maid-in-waiting was sent to the country to forget. Thus was born Anne Boleyn's hatred for Cardinal Wolsey.

CHAPTER 4

GOLDEN DAYS AT CHELSEA

The title "Speaker of the House" was worn well by Sir Thomas More. Henry VIII was quite ready to explain that he received the honor because of his "wit, learning and discretion." There were additional titles and grants as well. He was made High Steward of the University of Oxford and Cambridge, Collector of Subsidy in Middlesex and new titles were continually coming. These were "golden days" and Thomas More was the first to enjoy it. He moved his family to a large house in Chelsea, surrounded by a garden and farm. His property bordered the Thames River and even though close to the city, had all the greenness and seclusion of a country estate. "Here he was the firm ruler, the loving parent, the scholar, the philosopher, the best of hosts to a constant stream of guests."[2]

The King came more than once for a visit. Unannounced, and full of the unpredictable, he would tap on the door, delight in the surprise of the servants, and then rejoice in the genuine warmth of the greeting with which Sir Thomas welcomed him.

On this particular day, the sun was warm, but not hot, and the More garden was in full bloom. The two men walked casually back and forth totally unaware of anything other than the delightful conversation they were having. The King had familiarly draped his arm over More's shoulder, while the rest of More's family—wife, children, and son-in-law—pressed their noses against the back windows and watched with awe written all over their faces.

After the King left to pick up again the heavy weight of his office, the family clustered around Sir Thomas. Will Roper expressed the sentiments of the entire family. He was impressed and he told him so.

More smiled, "I have no cause to be proud," he said kindly, "for if my head would

[2] *The Story of Thomas More,* John Farrow; All Saints Press, p. 91

More's family watched
with awe written all over their faces.

win him a castle in France, it should not fail to go."

❀

The days at Chelsea were immortalized by the talented brush of the painter Holbein, who during his stay at Chelsea, painted Sir Thomas, a family portrait, and other individual portraits.

Chapter 5

1525 – A RESTLESS YEAR

Sir Thomas More was now forty-seven years old. Wolsey was fifty-two years old; Henry, thirty-four years of age; Catherine, forty years of age; Anne Boleyn, eighteen years old. The stage was almost set, the lights were dimming, the curtains began slowly to open on one of the most staggering events ever to dawn on the great drama of civilization.

The marriage of Henry and Catherine had resulted in the birth of a girl, Mary. There were other repeated miscarriages, but no other children came their way. England definitely was not in favor of the fact that a Queen should rule. Yet, Catherine had not produced a male heir to the throne, nor was it now probable that she would.

Thus was begun a problem which would be titled King Henry's "great matter." He said he doubted the validity of his marriage, because Catherine had first been married to his sickly older brother, Arthur. Catherine and Arthur had both been children and barely knew each other. After Arthur's death, the Pope had given a dispensation allowing Catherine to marry her dead husband's brother Henry. So, despite King Henry's "doubt," there was really no doubt that Catherine's marriage to Henry was valid and that her precious daughter Mary was the fruit of a valid marriage.

Sir Thomas More smelled the storm that was coming. One afternoon, he strolled with Roper along the shores of the Thames.

"Three things I would wish for Christendom," Sir Thomas was saying, "first, that where most of the Christian princes be at war, they instead would be at universal peace."

"Second," he continued, "that where the Church of Christ is, at present, sore and afflicted with errors and heresies, it will soon be settled in a perfect uniformity of religion."

"Third," ... and then he paused for a moment, in order to phrase his statement, "that where the king's matter of his marriage is now in question, that to the glory of God and quietness of all parties, it may be brought to a good conclusion."

But Henry's marriage problem was not as yet directly related to the life of Sir Thomas More, not nearly so directly as the heresies, which were so rampantly crossing the continent of Europe. The dedicated pen of Thomas More knew no boundaries of oceans or miles. He began to refute the great anti-Catholic minds of the day. Among them were William Tyndale and John Frith, who had been carried away with the new trend. Then there were Simon Fish and Christopher St. Germaine, two lawyers. It was four against one. But More did not fear the odds. His method was calm reasoning marked with humor. The first essay was "Dialogue against Heresies"; the second, "Quoth He and Quoth I"; the third, "Supplication of a Soul." And the battle of pens raged. More was winning thumbs down and the clergy were grateful.

Chapter 6

TRIAL IN BLACKFRIAR'S HALL

Cardinal Wolsey was tingling with ideas. Henry's appeal to Rome for a dispensation met only with delay.... And Henry was not one to accept delay—especially when his heart was infatuated with an enchanting young lady named Anne Boleyn. Henry turned to Wolsey for the solution. He came to a rather drastic solution. All the English Bishops were gathered to declare the marriage of Catherine to Henry invalid. The puffy Cardinal expected a quick affirmation, but a certain Bishop Fisher was quite outspoken. Queen Catherine made her appearance. She curtsied before her husband, then turned slowly to face the Bishops. Her voice was steady and determined as she said,
"I appeal to the Pope."

❋

Cardinal Campeggio was sent to England as the Papal Representative. The new trial was held in Blackfriar's Hall, London. The King on his throne, the assembled body of Bishops, the Papal Legate and the strong-faithed Catherine gathered. Most of the crowd of Bishops sympathized with Catherine, but their fear of Henry was stronger.

"No one comes forward any longer in the Queen's name," the Papal nuncio wrote to Rome.

Catherine, with full skirts rustling, knelt before her husband, and in the presence of an awe-struck audience, pleaded her cause,

"I have been a good and loyal wife," she said in her broken English. "I put it to your conscience." Turning to the court, she said, "To God I commit my cause."

Then, majestically, and with complete control, she left. Henry realized the emotional impact upon the Bishops that Catherine's words had caused. And so he began to talk in his soft and gentle way, persuading, pleading with the Assembly of Bishops. After all, this grave matter involved the secrets of conscience, the scruples of conscience. He asked the Bishops if they did not *all* agree. The spokesman rose.

"Yes," he said, "we will agree."

Then a voice with startling firmness rang throughout the room,

"No sir, not I. You have not *my* consent to it."

The courtroom turned to find the face that matched the voice. The face and the voice belonged to John Fisher, Bishop of Rochester.

"Look at this," the King said angrily, waving a piece of paper. "Isn't this your signature and seal?"

Fisher glanced furiously at his fellow Bishops and answered,

"No sir, it is not! I said to you I never would consent to such an act, for it is against my conscience."

The embarrassed spokesman admitted that he had forged the seal. There was an awful silence and then,

"Well, it doesn't matter," Henry said bluntly. "We won't argue with you, for you are but one man."

The trial continued. At least forty witnesses favored the King. The voice of Bishop Fisher rang out alone,

"Whom God has joined together, let no man put asunder."

Quite unpredictably, Cardinal Campeggio closed the trial and went to Rome, saying that it would continue there.

Chapter 7

WOLSEY WITHOUT THE RED

The trial had failed. Wolsey was white with fear for this had been his trial too—a test of his influence and strength. On October 9, he was removed as Lord Chancellor, for although the Church laws had been upheld in this matter, the King's wishes had been flustered. Now for Wolsey, the King was always placed before the Church. He, as the representative of Christ, should have upheld the law ... but this would mean prison and death. He, instead, decided to throw in his lot with secular princes, and knelt in front of Henry, begging for another chance. It was denied.

The Cardinal was exiled to Esher, his country home, while crowds screamed "Traitor" at the hated man. Anne Boleyn was delighted. Now he would pay ... for that old hurt in her life. Constantly she whispered into Henry's ear, prodding ... and suggesting....

In his country home, Wolsey could not relax. He expected trouble at any moment. And he did not have long to wait.

"My Lord, I arrest you for high treason," a man stormed at Wolsey. The words were spoken by none other than the gloating Earl of Northumberland, whose romance with Ann Boleyn had been crushed by the Cardinal.

Wolsey was ordered back to London for trial. By the evening of the third day he was terribly ill and stopped at an Augustinian Abbey. He was put to bed from which he never rose again.

Sensing that death was near, a much-humbled Wolsey made a general confession; and received the Last Sacraments. As the deeds of his life flashed through his mind again and again, he could only lament.

"If I had served God as diligently as I have the King, He would not have given me over in my old age."

The monks sang the beautiful Requiem Mass for a man who had so loved splendor and luxurious affairs. But no monument was put to mark his tomb and as fate would have it, to this day, the place of his burial is not known.

PART III

*"The Victory belongs to those
who think they can win."*

FATHER PLUS, S.J.

CHAPTER 1

NEW LORD CHANCELLOR

How to decide... how to pick a replacement for Wolsey. Few wanted an ecclesiastic. They wanted a layman, who was a scholar, a lawyer, an ambassador; a man who was not ambitious or self-seeking; one noted for his piety and orthodoxy as well. Incredible though it may seem, there was one man in England, who was all of this. Thomas More was given the "Great Seal" and proclaimed Lord Chancellor of England.

There was no duty that Sir Thomas desired less; but he plunged in with that dogged completeness, which he had developed since those early days at Oxford. Cases lay on his desk, which had been pending, some for as long as twenty years. More blew the dust off and cleared them up one by one. The day actually came when court officers informed him that there was no unfinished business. In fact a rhyme soon sprang up:

> "When More some time had Chancellor been,
> No more suits did remain;
> The same shall never more be seen
> Till More be there again."

His reputation for justice and honesty became a tradition. This may be symbolized in a little story. An old beggar lady came to the Lord Chancellor's court room and complained that her little dog had run away and been taken in by a wealthy lady. The poor old soul lamented that when she tried to get the puppy back, the servants refused to usher her into the lady's presence.

"Well, just who is this good woman?" More asked. "Perhaps they will let me see her."

"She is the wife of the Lord Chancellor," the lady smiled sweetly.

So Sir Thomas sent for his wife. Lady Alice and the dog appeared shortly. At one end of the courtroom stood Lady Alice. At the other, the beggar lady waited. The Lord Chancellor walked to the center of the room with the little dog wiggling in his arms.

The Lord Chancellor walked to the center of the room, the little dog wiggling in his arms.

"Now, whomever the dog goes to may keep it." The little puppy, set on the floor, dashed toward the old woman.

"It is yours," Sir Thomas said cheerfully.

The old lady was so amazed at his kindness that she made a gift of the dog to Lady Alice.

But all of the cases were not as easy to solve as that one. Say, for example, the marriage case of Henry VIII. Another Ambassador, Anne Boleyn's father, had been sent to Rome. The Pope hesitated ... he withheld a decision, hoping that the infatuation for Ann Boleyn would die, and with it, the marriage doubts. Henry grew angry. He fined the English clergy 400,000 crowns. The frightened clergy promptly raised the sum. Henry would not accept it unless they would declare him supreme head of the Church in England.

An increasing dilemma was rising for More. The words of the Gospel cut his conscience.

"Render therefore to Caesar the things that are Caesar's; and to God the things that are God's."

At this time, the Lord Chancellor should have strongly supported his king, but More was curiously silent.

Chapter 2

WHO SHALL HOLD THE KEYS: PETER OR THE KING?

King Henry had left Catherine for good. In fact, Anne had moved into the Queen's apartments. The whole situation was very unpopular throughout England and when the alluring Anne Boleyn appeared in public, crowds openly hissed.

On May 15, 1532, a document entitled "The Submission of the Clergy" was presented to Henry by the Archbishop of Canterbury. The Church in England had become the property of the King. The Clergy swore to make no move whatsoever, without royal consent.

The next day, Sir Thomas More resigned his office.

❋

Lady Alice sat in stunned silence. Not one of the family moved. They seemed scarcely to breathe as Sir Thomas unfolded a story of political and romantic intrigue—a story of a man, a King, who like all men of all times, had to choose between God and the world. This particular King chose the world; and because he was a man of great influence and responsibility, his choice would affect many other lives as well. Thomas More's life and career were radically changed by the King's decision. More had a lively and sensitive conscience. He knew that this choice would ultimately come: God or an erroneous King. He must choose God and pay for it with the wrath of his monarch. But the pains that might be inflicted by Henry were nothing compared to the pains that a guilty conscience can inflict. More chose to follow his conscience—a much narrower, yet safer way. And so began the game called "God versus the world." A game where results are certain and "chance" has no part—the conscience game.

CHAPTER 3

A VICTORY FOR EX-CHANCELLOR MORE

Sir Thomas could have resumed his law practice. Instead he took up his pen again, but now on a full-time scale. Most of the English clergy were so perplexed and anxious about the state of affairs within England, that they scarcely thought of Luther and the heresies raging abroad. But More did. He wrote a series of works at this time, which totalled almost half a million words.

And when the family conversation was flourishing, Thomas would lend his contribution. He began to speak much about the joys of heaven, the pains of hell, the martyrs... especially, yes, those martyrs, who died so gloriously, so thoroughly triumphant, for the Faith. They were fast becoming his favorite topics of conversation.

Now that his income was drastically reduced, Sir Thomas could no longer maintain the large staff of servants. But he did not just dismiss them. Instead, he found each one of them a job first. They were most unhappy about having to leave the joyful home of Thomas More. Only the Jester had the courage to joke about it.

"Chancellor More is Chancellor no more," he chided in sing-song tone. But then he wept like a child. The More jester was sent to continue his merry-making in the home of the Mayor of London.

As the family found itself with only the plainest of possessions, More invited them good-naturedly,

"Let's go abegging together."

But while Sir Thomas joked and kept his usual cheerful smile, Meg knew the sorrow, the worry, the pain that was eating his heart away.

"I worry for my wife and my children," he confided to Meg. "Sometimes I am awake an entire night ... thinking, fearful of what the King's wrath might do to you. Faith, Meg, a man needs faith. One could be utterly destroyed without it."

❂

Sir Thomas More refused the invitation to the marriage of King Henry VIII to Ann

Boleyn. He would not be present at the coronation either. The cunning eye of Ann Boleyn noticed his absence and she was angry.

A special committee appointed by the King summoned More to a court session to answer for his conduct on certain matters. To one accusation after another, he defended himself with admirable skill and the session was necessarily closed.

Meg was delighted with the victory. But her father, patting her on the shoulder, only replied:

"What is postponed is not abandoned."

CHAPTER 4

THE APPOINTMENT

News of Rome's pronouncement of the King's marriage as valid, the divorce of Catherine, and marriage to Anne Boleyn, the coronation of Anne Boleyn, despite the tears of a shocked English nation– these were mere passing events compared to the death blow which was soon coming.

The "Act of Succession" was passed by Henry VIII on March 23, 1534. It involved two things:

1) Declaring that Anne Boleyn's children would be the legitimate heirs to the throne.

2) Recognizing Henry VIII as head of the Church in England. A commission representing the King witnessed the oath of obedience. The Lords and Clergy were called first and then the laymen of high standing.

It was the Sunday after Easter. Sir Thomas and Roper had just attended morning Mass at St. Paul's and the summons came. More was to appear before the Committee the next day. It was his turn to take the oath.

The next morning, as he received the Master in Holy Communion, he struggled for the courage to go on with the game—that game of conscience.

Sad moments of "Good Bye" arrived, much sadder for More, because he knew that never again would he see his family as a free man; never again would he walk along the shores of the Thames River, or behold the family home in Chelsea. Lady Alice and the children never suspected the urgency of the situation, except Meg. The sadness lined on her father's face caused a stream of silent tears to slide down her cheeks. Only Roper, constant and faithful Roper, accompanied him down the sidewalk and through the streets to the dock. The journey was made in a small boat. There was total silence except for the steady beat of the oars. But even this sound went unnoticed, for Thomas More was deep in thought.

He went over the issue in his mind. He measured past events, and anticipated future ones. Then, soon enough, the wrinkled brow became smooth, and More appeared almost cheerful.

"Son," Sir Thomas addressed Roper, "I thank Our Lord the field is won."

Roper had no idea of the seriousness of the situation, when he responded casually,

"Sir, I am very glad."

Chapter 5

SO HIGH THE PRICE

Sir Thomas More entered the room and stood before the King's commission. He looked into the eyes of each man. They knew him, and he knew them. In fact, they even liked him ... and it was also a fact that he liked them. Of course, it was an equal fact that Thomas More liked everybody.

There were no dramatics; there were no demands. As a lawyer, More knew his rights. So he asked to see the document he was supposed to sign. He read it slowly and calmly, and then quietly, simply, he said,

"No, I cannot sign."

The commission was startled. The Oath-taking had been taken quite lightly by MOST. In fact, the majority of nobility were tripping over each other trying to be first in line. This was explained to More, but he only replied:

"They have their conscience. I have mine."

Sir Thomas was sent out into the garden for at least two hours to reconsider. As he paced among the flowers, which he loved so much, he witnessed a steady stream of clergy going in to sign. Many joked and laughed as they waited.

The same day another man refused to sign as well. His name was Father Nicholas Wilson. He was immediately led to the prison known as "the Tower."

All the while, More paced the garden, not searching for a decision, for he knew his answer, but thinking and preparing for the consequences, which would result: death, the suffering of his family, the possible long ordeal of torture.

When the commission asked again for his answer, it was a firm and determined "No."

Sir Thomas More was kept in custody at Westminster Abbey. Henry just could not admit him to the tower. But Anne insisted, pleaded, nagged....

CHAPTER 6

THE TOWER

It was Friday, April 17, 1535. Thomas More found himself committed to the tower. The jailor, who met him, apologized for the wretchedness of the place, but More only joked it off. His cell was damp, dark and dirty. This was sacrifice enough and yet he still wore the hairshirt. Perhaps it was worn for some special intention, known only to himself.

There were certain privileges that he was allowed...luxuries, you might say, such as pen, paper and a daily walk. It wasn't much to compensate for the man who had been Lord Chancellor. The poor jailor was very embarrassed; yet, More was completely happy. He didn't expect any more.

Immediately he began the first letter to Meg.

"Since I have come here by my own choice," he began, "I trust that God by His goodness, will discharge me of my care, and, with His gracious help, supply my lack among you...."

Then he came to the part which caused him to fumble and falter. It was obvious that More was deliberately choosing death, and he tried to explain the "why's" of it to his family.

"I may tell you, Meg, that they have committed me here, for refusing to take the Oath, not agreeable with the Law, and are not able to justify my imprisonment...."

❋

Meg was allowed to come for an occasional visit. The first time that she actually saw her father behind bars and realized the significance of the situation, she cried, and begged, really begged her father to sign the Act, as the rest were doing. Words would not come to him. He had so much to say, but all of his efforts reached only as far as his lips and then froze in icy silence. Only after she left did he break, and muffled sobs filled the cell.

Yet, almost immediately, he penned a letter to Meg, trying to capture the thoughts of his soul:

"None of the terrible things that might happen to me touched me so grievously as to see you, my well-beloved child, in such pitious

She cried and begged.... Words would not come to him.

manner, labor to persuade me about the thing, which I have of pure necessity, for respect for my own soul, often given you so precise an answer."

When his wife begged him to return to their home in Chelsea, he looked around his dank cell and asked:

"Is not this house as near heaven as my own?"

CHAPTER 7

MAKING AND BREAKING

Months passed and the screws were tightened. Now there was no more afternoon walk. The chaplain was no longer permitted to visit. Even his pen and paper were taken from him. Meg's letters were now written with hunks of charcoal on whatever material he could find.

*

A note was delivered to Thomas More's cell. Its shaky handwriting was from a man who had been confined the same day as More. Father Wilson wondered if there wasn't some sort of a compromise possible. More answered that he could only form his own opinion and follow his own conscience. Wilson wrote back that he had decided to take the Oath.

More, with a hunk of charcoal, on a bit of scrap paper, wrote back, without even a hint of criticism,

"I beseech Our Lord give you good luck ... leaving every other man to his own conscience, myself, with God's grace, will follow my own. Remember me in your devout prayers, and I shall remember you in mine, such as they be."

•

The situation was growing hotter each day. Once, while Meg visited Sir Thomas, a group of Carthusians passed by his cell window on the way to their death.

"Your old dad will have to wait longer than they for heaven, Meg, for I have led a useless and foolish life. They are ready for heaven; I am not."

But Thomas More was closer to heaven than he knew.

CHAPTER 8

CARDINAL FISHER

John Fisher, the Bishop of Rochester, was another distinguished guest in the tower. He would not sign the Act of Succession either. His Holiness, Pope Paul III raised the brave bishop to the dignity of a cardinal, hoping that perhaps this would help to save his life.

Henry VIII had a ready reply,

"While I cannot permit a cardinal's hat to be brought to England, I will be glad to arrange for Fisher's head to be sent to Rome, instead."

Fisher and More were now Henry's principal targets. They were continually examined and cross-examined. Every trick was employed to get an open and verbal denial from each of them that the King was head of the Church in England.

Richard Rich, an agent of Henry, asked Fisher's opinion, swearing secrecy, because it was only to relieve the King's conscience. Rich then went to court with the needed evidence.

The trial in Westminster Hall was only a formality. The verdict was pronounced long before the courageous Cardinal ever stepped into the courtroom. He was given the death sentence and it was scheduled for five days later. Led to the scaffold on June 22, Cardinal Fisher, after his torturous imprisonment, was so thin, so gaunt, that one man described him as,

"Death in a man's shape, and using a man's voice."

The people had to learn what happened to men who disobeyed the King. The Cardinal's body was thrown in a shallow grave and his head was placed on London Bridge.

Still More stood firm.

CHAPTER 9

PERSUASION

One thing in this whole amazing story is quite certain. Henry VIII really didn't want to put More to death. Instead, he wanted him only to sign the Oath. Death would not help in this situation. He really loved More, and so he kept trying one more means of persuasion.

All of London's most influential men were called in, and one by one, they visited More's cell. They tried every clever approach, but More's answer was always the same,

"The Law is like a two-edged sword. If I should speak against it, I shall procure the death of my body. If I should consent to it, I shall procure the death of my soul."

❋

Now, More was not even permitted the pleasure of reading. All books were removed from his cell. His time was spent in prayer and meditation. The trial was near and he begged for the strength. He could not quit now. After weeks of being cooped up in a damp cell, his health was poor. He could not even take a step without fumbling. His once broad shoulders were now terribly stooped, and his weight was reduced to a shadow.

The trial was July 1. Dressed in a rough gown, More was dragged through the most populated streets. Contempt must be shown for the man who dared disobey the King. But there was NO contempt shown that day. There was awe and admiration in the crowds as the broken man passed by. Nameless voices wished him well and promised to pray for him. Others sobbed at the terrible shock of seeing one of the most beloved men of England, the champion of the common man, reduced to such a state. His body was broken, but his mind was as keen as ever.

There wasn't one man on the jury that More did not know. How they dreaded this moment . . . this trial, above all others. More did not look at a man; he looked through him. As the indictment was read, Lawyer More calmly and brilliantly cleared himself on every charge. Even the perjury of Mr. Rich was proven by More to be just what it was. And yet, the verdict came. Sentence was pronounced slowly and solemnly,

"Guilty; death...."

This was the moment that he had feared—feared not the condemnation but that he would not have the courage to take it well. But the grace had come when it was needed.

"I forgive you," he said to his judges. The words were sincere, almost friendly. "I forgive you as Stephen forgave Saul. And just as now both are holy saints in heaven and shall continue there friends together forever, so I trust and pray that, though your Lordships have been on earth my Judges of condemnation, we may meet hereafter merrily together in heaven."

Tears were their only reply.

8. Conscience Game

CHAPTER 10

THE LONGEST ROAD

A procession formed to take the condemned man back to the tower. Crowds of sympathizers stood by. Silence was everywhere. As they moved in the direction of the prison, John, the youngest of the More family, pushed through the crowd and kneeling at his father's feet, buried his head against his body. Kingston, the jailor, wept so loudly that Sir Thomas had to console him.

When the group arrived at the gate of the prison, a lone figure waited there. A woman... who ignored the crowd, the jailor, the soldiers. She saw only the prisoner in a ragged brown habit.

"Oh Dad," she cried, "Dad." Meg flung her arms about her father's neck and kissed him again and again. This moment for More took more courage than any trial's verdict.

"Whatever I suffer," he whispered gently as he held her face in his hands, "is God's will...."

"Whatever I suffer," he whispered gently as he held her face in his hands, "is God's will. Do you believe that, Meg?" He blessed her and held her just for a moment. Then it was time to move on. As Sir Thomas continued his lonely walk, Meg, overcome with the depth of love for her father, rushed up to him again, and squeezing him tightly, pressed one last kiss to his cheek. More had no response to this impulsive gesture. For once in his life the words were not there.

※

His rough piece of charcoal was busily engaged in writing farewell notes. The last letter was sent to Meg. And a gift went with it—the hair shirt, that familiar form of penance and mortification.

Chapter 11

VICTORY – JULY 6, 1535

The man who mounted the scaffold on that sultry July morning, did not think of himself as a martyr. In fact, that he would ever be listed as such, or be honored on the calendar of saints, would have made him laugh for sure. There was nothing glorious or extraordinary about this event in his mind. He was just a man, following his conscience, playing the game of life according to that conscience.

Another man that same morning was playing a different kind of game. Henry VIII was having a game of cards with Ann Boleyn. The King was obviously preoccupied. Anne began to pry. Her husband blurted suddenly,

"You are the cause of this man's death." He stormed out of the room and spent hours alone.

Sir Thomas More was told to speak briefly at the death scene. He obeyed. His speech was only a sentence length. It was directed to his wife, to his children, to Roper, to the throngs who loved him. It was directed above all to Meg. The motive for his death; the reason for it....

"I die, the King's good servant, but God's first."

DAUGHTERS OF ST. PAUL

In Massachusetts
    50 St. Paul's Avenue
        Boston, Mass. 02130
    172 Tremont Street
        Boston, Mass. 02111
    381 Dorchester Street
        So. Boston, Mass. 02127
    325 Main Street
        Fitchburg, Mass. 01420

In New York
    78 Fort Place
        Staten Island, N.Y. 10301
    625 East 187th Street
        Bronx, N.Y. 10458
    525 Main Street
        Buffalo, N.Y. 14203

In Connecticut
    202 Fairfield Avenue
        Bridgeport, Conn. 06603

In Ohio
    141 West Rayen Avenue
        Youngstown, Ohio 44503
    415 Euclid Avenue
        Cleveland, Ohio 44114

In Florida
    2700 Biscayne Blvd.
        Miami, Florida 33137

In Louisiana
    2814 South Carrollton Avenue
        New Orleans, La. 70118
    86 Bolton Avenue
        Alexandria, La. 71301

In Texas
    114 East Main Plaza
        San Antonio, Texas 78205

In California
    1570 Fifth Avenue
        San Diego, Calif. 92101
    278 - 17th Street
        Oakland, Calif. 94612

In Canada
    8885 Blvd. Lacordaire
    St. Leonard Deport-Maurice
        Montreal, Canada
    1063 St. Clair Avenue West
        Toronto, Canada

In Australia
    58 Abbotsford Road
        Homebush N.S.W., Australia

In Africa
    Box 4392
        Kampala, Uganda

In England
    29 Beauchamp Place
        London, S.W. 3, England

In India
    Water Field Road Extension
    Plot N. 143
        Bandra, India

In Philippine Islands
    No. 326 Lipa City
        Philippine Islands